Kai Hilpisch

English in Japanese Language and Culture

A Socio-Historical Analysis

Kai Hilpisch

English in Japanese Language and Culture

A Socio-Historical Analysis

GRIN Verlag

Bibliografische Information der Deutschen Nationalbibliothek: Die Deutsche Bibliothek
verzeichnet diese Publikation in der Deutschen Nationalbibliografie; detaillierte bibliografische Daten sind im Internet über http://dnb.d-nb.de/ abrufbar.

1. Auflage 2009
Copyright © 2009 GRIN Verlag
http://www.grin.com/
Druck und Bindung: Books on Demand GmbH, Norderstedt Germany
ISBN 978-3-640-47115-7

Kai-Victor Hilpisch

ENGLISH IN JAPANESE LANGUAGE AND CULTURE: A SOCIO-HISTORICAL ANALYSIS

Bachelor Thesis

Course of Studies: *Language and Communication & Literary, Cultural and Media Studies*

University of Siegen, 2009

AUTHOR'S PREFACE ON THE ONLINE-VERSION OF THIS TEXT

Dear Reader,

this bachelor thesis has been submitted at Siegen University in August, 2009, and was later graded 1.0. With this thesis, I completed my studies for a *Bachelor of Arts in Language & Communication and Literary, Cultural and Media Studies*. As of now, I am enrolled in a master's programme for applied linguistics.

Feel free to use this thesis as a source, but please use proper citation and give bibliographical information when using my ideas.

Also, please feel encouraged to contact me about any questions you have or errors you might have spotted – my knowledge of Japanese is restricted, thus I am aware that there might be errors or inaccuracies, especially with the translations, and I would like to correct those at some point.

I hope this thesis can be helpful to students interested in Japanese language and culture. This thesis can be considered an introduction to the topic, for more thorough exploration of this field, please refer to the bibliography, especially Stanlaw (2004).

Kai Hilpisch

1st of November, 2009

Table of contents

1. Introduction

トヨタ　の　サラリマン　わ　ネクタイ　と　ソフトアイスカリム　を　かいます。

Were it not for the foreign scripture, the above Japanese sentence could be understood at least vaguely by the majority of speakers of the English language. Transcribed in *romaji*, the way of writing Japanese with Roman characters, the sentence reads:

toyota no sarariman wa nekutai to sofutoaisukarimu o kaimasu.

If this sentence is dissected, one will probably first notice the famous name *Toyota*, well-known for decades of motorized transportation. However, three more words in that sentence are actually known if one looks more closely. Pronouncing the sentence aloud multiple times may help to discover that *sarariman* is *salary man, nekutai* is *necktie* and *sofutoaisukarimu* is *soft-ice-cream*. Now, at least the most probable sentence subject (the salary man), and the objects are clear. Given that one has at least a rudimentary knowledge of Japanese, *kaimasu* translates to *to buy,* and now one can understand what the sentence is about: a typical office worker is buying another necktie and a cold snack. The few words that could not be translated are probably the grammatical items: *no* meaning *from*, *wa* marks the subject or sentence-topic, *to* means *and* and *o* marks an accusative relationship to the sentence-final verb.

Although, admittedly, of slightly obscure content, the example sentence could have been uttered in a perfectly normal Japanese conversation. Present-day Japanese is full of foreign loanwords, and everyday communication is virtually impossible without relying on a huge variety of loans, mostly from English. "According to Japanese statistical surveys, English 'loanwords' and phrases account for between 5 and 10 percent of the daily Japanese vocabulary" (Stanlaw, 2004 : 1), letting the number of anglicisms in, for example, German pale in comparison[1]. Even though various groups fear the loss of a substantial amount of Japanese identity due to excessive borrowing (Stanlaw, 2004 : 273), it is a fact that Western items of any variety and description have entered the Japanese vocabulary during the past century with the speed and proportions of a landslide. Walking down a street in a shopping district of any Japanese city, one will notice that among the innumerable signs and adverts there is a huge

---

[1] Ulrich Busse examined the number of loanwords found in volumes of German "DUDEN"-dictionaries (which are considered the 'standard' of German vocabulary) and concluded that the percentage of loanwords rose from 1.36% to only 3.46% between 1880 and 1986 (see "Deutsche Sprachgeschichte vom Spätmittelalter bis zur Gegenwart", Vol. 3, Peter von Polenz, de Gruyter 1999, p. 402)

3

amount of western letters, which can be found right next to Japanese script. They come as initials like *DVD*, national and international brand names (*Sony* or *Nike*) and in slogans as well (*I'm lovin' it!*). This shows that English has an enormous presence in commercial contexts, implying that the average Japanese customer has sufficient proficiency in written English for the advertising to be effective. The use of English also extends into Japanese popular culture. The music industry heavily relies on English, as can be seen to some extent if one looks at the Japanese Top 20[2] in 2009, revealing that the whole list consists of either songs by (mostly American) international artists, or songs by Japanese artists with completely English titles or titles that at least contain some English loans.

One might want to conclude from the above examples that there is a generally high proficiency of English in Japan. This impression is supported by the very organized and thorough approach to ESL, with an average of six years of English education in the overall strictly organized and high-level educational system. However, as Stanlaw points out, even though "the popularity of English has risen dramatically, [...] this has found greatest expression not in the creation of large groups of [...] 'near-native' speakers of the language, but rather through the nativization of English loanwords [...] within the Japanese language system" (2004 : 81-82). This means that although the Japanese are able to recognize a wide range of English words, these are mostly nativized loanwords and are not treated as part of an actual foreign language. English proficiency for purposes of international communication, gained through school and college training, is often considered insufficient; for example "74.9 percent of college graduates evaluated their English instruction in Japan negatively" (Koike, et al., 1995 : 19) in a General Survey of English Language Teaching conducted between 1983 and 1990.

Still, in spite of their lack in proficiency, the Japanese appear to be very fond of English – but apparently, only the language, not the people who speak it. The Japanese attitude towards foreigners can of course only be described as very polite, but ultimately, foreigners are always treated as outsiders, even if they have been residents of Japan for decades or even generations. For example, "many Americans are infuriated by their ultimate rejection and irritated by the unconsciously pejorative overtones of words used for foreigners" (Reischauer, et al., 1995 : 400). Early obviously impolite terms like *ijin* (*strange people*) and *keto* (*hairy barbarians*) may have been removed from official and most of everyday language, but the now prevalent

---

[2] For an example see [http://top40-charts.com/chart.php?cid=16]

politically correct term *gaijin* still shows what most non-Japanese are seen as: *outsiders*. This strongly contrasts with the excessive use of foreign loans in Japanese and the general interest in Western cultural items, creating a paradoxical situation: how can a culture that puts such strong emphasis on its seclusion from the rest of the world be so fond of the language spoken by much of the very same world?

In this paper, the history of English-Japanese language contact will be described and how the current status of English in Japan was established. Also taken into consideration are both socio-historical developments in politics, economy and the media, as well as the vivid history of language contact Japan has to offer; also with other languages than English. This paper will begin with a thorough history of Japan's encounters with foreigners as well as their languages, then continue with a detailed description of the status of English in today's Japanese culture and conclude with an analysis of the status of loanwords in Japanese culture and the concept of *wa-sei eigo*, the so-called *English-made-in-Japan*. This thesis' intention is to show the connections between a long history of international language contact, English education and socio-historical factors and how these resulted in today's Japanese variety of English.

2. History of Japanese-English language contact

Japans history of language contact is unique in multiple ways. First, it is characterized by interchanging periods of seclusion (first geographically, then politically) and relative openness to other cultures. In a comparably short period of time, the secluded island-country made a huge turn "from internalization – being internally oriented – toward internationalization" (Koike, et al., 1995 : 14). This was strongly driven by economic developments: "the Japanese economy in 1988 was nine times its size in real GNP [Gross National Product] in 1955" (Koike, et al., 1995 : 14). In less than a century, a nation changed from a system of feudal lords and prevalent seclusion from anything 'outside' to one of the world's leading economic forces, especially through export. The internationalization resulted in a rising demand for English education, which led to quick developments in both the school system and on the private sector. Today, English is practically compulsory in most Japanese schools and effectively an entrance requirement for most colleges (Koike, et al., 1995 : 17). Furthermore, Japanese businessmen and women are eager to participate in additional English courses, since higher proficiency greatly improves the chances for promotion (Morrow, 1995 : 87).

The second unique aspect is related specifically to English-Japanese language contact. The contact with English speaking foreigners resulted not in one, but two pidgins. A pidgin is a simplified language system that may evolve when two groups of different origin are in need to communicate without having a common linguistic base – they will create one of their own, a so-called pidgin language (Sebba, 1997 : 13-15). A pidgin comes with a reduced set of grammatical rules and vocabulary, mostly restricted to the topic at hand: trade and everyday needs. Usually, one party's language becomes the dominant one, contributing most of the grammar and structural items to the new pidgin, while the other language primarily just contributes further vocabulary items. Concerning this, Japanese-English language contact is not only unique because two different pidgins developed at two different points in history, but also because these pidgins differ very much in their basic structures: the first pidgin, the so-called Yokohama Dialect, was dominated by Japanese structures, while the second pidgin, Bamboo English, was based on English structures.

In this chapter, a chronological overview of the different periods of language contact in which Japan was involved will be given. At the same time, an explanation of how these periods are related to socio-historical developments in the country will be discussed. Starting with early (non-English) language contact, the aforementioned pidgins will be explored and the chapter will be concluded with a description of the transitional period, to lead on towards the next chapter on contemporary use of English in Japan.

2.1 Early language contact

Centuries before Westerners arrived at Japanese shores the Japanese had already established contact with other Asian countries. According to Coulmas (1989 : 122), it was through a Korean scholar that Chinese writing, the characters later to be called *kanji*, were introduced to Japan. Over time, the Japanese introduced changes to the syntax of written Chinese to make it usable as a means to transcribe Japanese, but not until the introduction of the *kana* syllabaries, especially *hiragana*, a natural transcription of spoken Japanese was possible (Coulmas, 1989 : 129). Before that, Chinese writing became one foundation of Japanese culture: it was *kanbun*, an often grammatically abnormal form of Chinese, which became the dominant means of written communication concerning scholarship, religion and literature, comparable to the status of Latin in Europe (Coulmas, 1989 : 123). While English is considered by many the language that moved Japan into the 20th century, it was Chinese which propelled it out of late Stone Age. The influence of Chinese culture, knowledge and technology "led to a shift from a

6

nomadic, tribal society to a settled, agrarian one" (Loveday, 1996 : 30). During this process, first borrowings occurred, and although there are no reliable resources from the time, many terms related to the innovations brought by the Chinese are suggested, such as agricultural terms like *shio* (*salt*), *ine* (*rice*) and *mugi* (*wheat*) as well as society-related ones like *sato* (*village*), *kuni* (*state*) and *haka* (*grave*) (Loveday, 1996 : 30).

While English is the most dominant Western contributor to the Japanese language today, its strong influence only started in the 1850s when the American commodore Matthew Perry re-opened the islands after two hundred years of self-imposed seclusion (Stanlaw, 2004 : 49). Before that, English only played a minor role among other European languages, namely the tongues of the big trading nations of the sixteenth century: Portuguese, Spanish and Dutch. Being the leading mercantile nation, Portugal made the first lasting linguistic impression on Japan after reaching the country in 1544. Stanlaw explains (2004 : 46), that the Portuguese not only brought "European-style mercantilism, but also Christianity, which was soon established in Japan", resulting in two percent of the Japanese population being converted by 1600. Besides economical and cultural influences, Portuguese also "evidently gave Japan its first European loanwords, many of which are still in use today" (Stanlaw, 2004 : 46):

Japanese	Portuguese	English
pan	*pão*	*bread*
kappa	*capa*	*raincoat, slicker*
rasha	*raxa*	*cloth*
tempura	*tempero*	*food fried in batter*
tabako	*tobaco*	*tobacco*

According to Stanlaw (2004 : 46), these first borrowings established many processes that became very productive in the process of nativization, for example the combination of a loanword with a Japanese prefix or suffix, as in *rasha-men*, affixing the Japanese word for *cotton*, *men* 綿. This literally meant *cotton-cloth*, but was often used to refer to women who "covered" themselves with foreign men later. Until 1637, borrowing from Portuguese and Spanish continued, but due to European quarrels spilling over into Japan and the various intrigues the Catholic missionaries were involved in, Japan felt the need for consequences (Stanlaw, 2004 : 47): Christianity was banned, Japanese converts who refused to give up the religion were killed and most Europeans were expelled from the country. Thus began the *sakoku*, a self-imposed isolation enabled by the Tokugawa regiment, to protect Japan from negative foreign influences (Dettmer, 1973 : 105).

There were, however, some exceptions to the *sakoku*. Besides contact to the Asian continent, there was still contact to Europe via the Dutch traders. This contact was "restricted to the small artificial island of Dejima in Nagasaki Bay" (Stanlaw, 2004 : 47), but the bi-annual visits of the Dutch traders were an important chance for the shogun and Japanese scholars to gain access to information on world affairs and new developments. According to Stanlaw (2004 : 47), the linguistic aspects of these encounters were managed by the so-called *oranda-tsuuji* (*Dutch interpreters*), who also served as customs officials. Dutch was the only Western language that was allowed to be studied during the *sakoku* and the *oranda-tsuuji* were the only ones who were given this privilege. These scholars also observed the Dutch doctors and occasionally conversed with them to gain insight on Western medicine. This unofficial interest became the foundation of *ran-gaku* (*Dutch Studies*), the study of Western science and medicine during the isolation. This field was expanded when shogun Tokugawa Yoshimune lifted some of the bans established by his predecessor and allowed the importing of books containing secular knowledge, thus enabling the *oranda-tsuuji* to expand their knowledge of the Dutch language together with other topics, resulting in the first Dutch-Japanese dictionary in 1796. Some Dutch traders even tried to learn Japanese, "a practice forbidden one hundred years earlier" (Stanlaw, 2004 : 48) and still dependent on the local authorities. Nevertheless, a considerable number of Dutch loanwords entered the Japanese vocabulary during the sakoku and many everyday terms are still used today (Stanlaw, 2004 : 48):

Japanese	Dutch	English
garasu	glas	glass
miruku	melk	milk
koohii	koffie	coffee

The influence of Dutch on the Japanese vocabulary does not only show in new nouns, but also in grammatical items. According to Stanlaw (2004 : 48), many linguists observed a rising frequency in the use of pronouns in standard Japanese, a language comparably free of pronouns. This might have been triggered by the direct translations from pronoun-rich Western languages, even resulting in the invention of new pronouns like *tokoro no* to deal easier with common relative clauses in Western languages (Miura, 1979 : 22). Dutch also had a huge impact on written Japanese, when the *oranda-tsuuji* noticed the close resemblance between spoken and written Dutch. It appeared as a stark contrast to diglossic Japan where the writing system based on Chinese characters forced writers to compose written Japanese in a totally different way than the spoken vernacular (Stanlaw, 2004 : 48). Translations originating from

Dutch texts showed "a comparably plain register of Japanese, an innovation that shook accepted literary traditions" (Stanlaw, 2004 : 49), which makes Dutch influence one of the initiating factors for later written language reforms.

The early contact with European languages already shows the open-mindedness of the Japanese towards anything Western; even the strong restrictions of international contact during the *sakoku* could not stop the stream of cultural and linguistic items assimilated into Japan. But this only foreshadowed the later processes of intercultural contact, which started to gain momentum with the arrival of the Americans.

2.2 The Yokohama dialect

According to Stanlaw (2004 : 49-50) English was rarely heard in Japan during the roughly 200 years of *sakoku* – save for a few exceptions, of course. One incident involved a British ship entering Nagasaki harbour under a Dutch flag, followed by a raid of storehouses and later the suicide of Nagasaki's magistrate commissioner to take responsibility for the incident. The negotiations with the intruders once more made fluency in English a valuable skill for the *oranda-tsuuji* of the already weakening *Tokugawa* regime. Much input came from Japanese Nakahama Manjiro, a fisherman's son who acquired near-native skills in English since he spent ten years in the USA after being rescued by an American whaler from ship wreckage. A few years later, an adventurous American by the name of Ranald MacDonald intentionally went the other way round, as he reached the coast of Japan in a small life-boat, pretending to be the victim of a ship wreckage The *oranda-tsuuji* "were overjoyed at gaining access to a 'native speaker' of English" (Stanlaw, 2004 : 50), since even during the *sakoku*, they continued their study of English and other foreign languages, if only for defensive measures. Their efforts culminated in the 'Official Office for the Translation of Barbarian Books into Japanese', an organized translation bureau which to some extent still exists today, after various renaming and restructuring, at the famous Tokyo University (Stanlaw, 2004 : 52). The institution also was the first example of government-sponsored education, showing how curiosity and competitiveness concerning the West led to reforms and innovations in Japan, often even without the direct influence of foreigners.

In 1853, the *sakoku* was effectively ended with the arrival of Commodore Perry and a squadron of American ships, forcing Japan to join "the world of 'civilized nations'" (Stanlaw, 2004 : 53) and securing America a favoured position as a trading partner as well as a safe haven in Japan. The Japanese representatives saw no choice to counter the 'invasion' of the Americans (and later various European countries) but by making contracts with the foreigners, even against the emperor's will (Dettmer, 1973 : 116). This resulted in the *Kanagawa* treaty with the Americans and later the *Ansei (five-power)* treaty with the U.S., Great Britain, Russia, France and the Netherlands (Dettmer, 1973 : 115). "The ports of Yokohama, Nagasaki and Hakodate were opened in 1859" and a rising fear of the Western influence turned some Japanese into "committed xenophobes" (Stanlaw, 2004 : 56). The Tokugawa government, already weakened, could not deal with the Western threat effectively and was replaced by Emperor *Meiji* in 1868, whose government immediately set various reforms into motion almost overnight – these changes in nearly every part of Japanese life are known as the Meiji Restoration or the Meiji Enlightenment, and an integral part of the reforms was the establishing of compulsory education with a curriculum in which English played an important role; often both as "the medium as well as the subject of instruction" (Stanlaw, 2004 : 56). But even though the new government had realized the importance of English (or rather, the West) to modernize Japan, it would take at least a decade until English language education was showing results. Thus, in the meantime, the growing numbers of Westerners entering Japan needed to be dealt with differently. The situation asked for a simple means of communication to enable both the foreigners and the Japanese to go about daily life and business immediately. It did not take long, as usual when money is at stake, to find a suitable way to communicate: the Yokohama dialect.

Yokohama was the first port that was opened to world trade, and soon enough a manifold selection of Westerners bustled about in the city. Quickly, they developed a pidginized Version of Japanese English, the so-called Yokohama dialect (Stanlaw, 2004 : 57). The pidgin was already extinct by the middle of the twentieth century, so written records are the only source of information regarding how communication worked in Yokohama and what the dialect sounded like. One of the most useful resources is a pamphlet called 'Exercises in the Yokohama Dialect' by Hoffman Atkinson, "a long-term resident in the Yokohama foreign settlement" (Stanlaw, 1987 : 94). The text was not designed to be a scientific resource but rather as a humorous insight into the emerging contact between Japan and its foreign guests. The most notable feature of the 'Exercises' is the way Atkinson used English words as a means of transcribing the phonetic features of Japanese expressions, often choosing intentionally humorous correlates (Stanlaw, 2004 : 57-58):

English	Atkinson	Japanese
good day	*ohio*	*o-hayoo*
church, temple	*oh terror*	*o-tera*
nine (9)	*coconuts*	*kokono-tsu*

In spite of the rather 'recreational' aims of Atkinson's text, he still supplied linguists with a comparably huge amount of data on the properties of the Yokohama dialect. Most importantly, it showed that at least 80-85 percent of the vocabulary came from Japanese, reflecting the ratio of native speakers of Japanese and English in the country. At the time, Westerners were mostly visitors rather than permanent residents: Yokohama was "home to some 1,500 Westerners, 3,000 Chinese and 25,000 Japanese" (Stanlaw, 2004 : 57). The Yokohama Dialect also utilized the complex system of honorifics in Japanese, notably preferring "self-deprecatory versions instead of neutral forms" (Stanlaw, 1987 : 95) on both sides. While Japanese contributed most verbs and nouns concerning everyday life, the English items reflect the influence of the Westerners and how concepts of internationalization became important (Stanlaw, 2004 : 58):

Japanese items	English items
mado (window)	*consul (consul)*
akai (red)	*hotel (hotel)*
ichi (one)	*curios (curiosities, 'things Japanese')*
muzukashii (difficult)	*house (home ,residence, building, store)*

Many English terms are related to the growing foreign community, and many terms did undergo semantic shift, as can be seen in the multiple meanings of *house*. Similar semantic extension can be observed with other items as well, such as *sacky* (derived from *sake*, Japanese rice-wine), which served as a descriptive for any kind of alcoholic beverage, including *beer sacky, akai (red) sacky* and the more obscure *square-face sacky*, which refers to a gin bottle with a typical square shape (Stanlaw, 2004 : 59). The speakers of English also contributed items inadvertently when their speech habits were observed by the Japanese. The word *kameya*, referring to the Western breeds of dogs the traders occasionally brought with them, is derived from the owners calling *come here* to their dogs, which was misinterpreted by the observing Japanese as the word for the animal itself.

Yokohama dialect usage was mostly restricted to the very port it originated from and other trading intersections. Its speakers were mainly merchants and traders who had little time and interest to learn each other's native language, since they were busy dealing with everyday matters. For the upper classes and the regime of Meiji-reformed Japan, however, English gained a highly prestigious value, since in the constant strive for modernization, "English replaced Dutch as the language to learn about the West. [...] The Meiji administration brought in a whole cadre of 'foreign experts' to instantly modernize the country [including] many official teachers of English, as well as others who offered their linguistic expertise for fee or favour" (Stanlaw, 2004 : 59). The importance of the Yokohama dialect declined until it vanished, but it left a lasting impression on the Japanese language as many loans which developed during that period persisted for a couple of decades or even until today.

2.3 Rise of English

The Yokohama dialect was not the only pidgin language that developed at the time. Seemingly, for every major aspect of life in Japan where contact between natives and foreigners was imminent, a speech developed with a set of items and rules restricted to the topic at hand. Stanlaw (2004 : 60) lists various semi-languages like 'nurse-talk', 'merchant-talk', 'driver-talk', 'brothel-talk' and 'sailor-talk', but beside these practically-inspired varieties, there also developed more professionally motivated Japanese attempts at the English language, such as the early textbook-inspired 'Interpreter's English' and the contents of various phrasebooks.

All the while, English became more and more fashionable among the nation's elite, together with the Western lifestyle in general. Students and the so-called *haikara* people fancied the West, emulating its ways – including the clothing. *Haikara* is a loan derived from *high-collar*, referring to Western fashion. English was deemed an important aspect of Western culture and thus it became a habit among students "to intersperse their daily conversation with English borrowings" (Stanlaw, 2004 : 60) as a sign for sophistication. A few samples of such speech are shown below; sentences from a conversation between Meiji university students taken from an 1875 novel Stanlaw cites (2004 : 61). English items are highlighted.

1. *Webster no daijiten – jitsu-ni kore wa **yuusufuru** ja.*
    This ,**Webster's** Comprehensive Dictionary' is really **useful**.
2. *Ningen no tanoshimi wa ani **sekkusu** nomi naruya.*
    Man's only pleasure is **sex**.
3. *Fragility. The name is woman.*
    Fragility [sic, 'frailty' from Hamlet, Act I, Scene 1] **thy name is woman**.

This kind of usage utilizes English as something fanciful, without any apparent sensible reason but one: to speak English was to be educated, to be modern, or even daring. In addition to that, more and more English-speaking foreigners entered Japan, most of them experts in one way or another, working as teachers or consultants in various fields. "These people did not speak Japanese and had little desire to learn it" (Stanlaw, 2004 : 61), forcing the Japanese interested in the mostly English lectures of these experts to become proficient in the Western tongue. Not only were most lectures held in English, written materials were usually imported from the West as well (Stanlaw, 2004 : 61). The government tried to support the enthusiastic learners in their country with a thorough reform of educational policy – by actually establishing one, since formal education had usually been a luxury of the upper classes in the pre-Meiji era. "As early as 1871, the fourth year of the Restoration, the government founded the Ministry of Education" (Koike, et al., 1995 : 16), which then quickly initiated a nationwide educational system. At the core of the new curriculum was a total of six years of English instruction for boys (a second foreign language was also compulsory in the final two years). English lessons at girls' schools followed later. Initially, large numbers of foreign teachers were hired to help Japan "to catch up with the advanced civilization of the Western world […] but by 1890 most foreign teachers were replaced by the Japanese ones" (Koike, et al., 1995 : 16). After the initial phase of 'catching up', the situation changed a little due to a rise of nationalism at the very end of the 19th century. The pressure to "emphasize […] Japanese culture and language […] undermined the policy of encouraging foreign language teaching" (Koike, et al., 1995 : 17), resulting in the abolishment of secondary foreign language courses and a general decrease in English lessons.

The Japanese were very enthusiastic learners of English, and there were many Westerners who tried to master the Japanese language in turn. Stanlaw argues that "there were a number of contact languages in use, both Japanese-based as well as English-based" (2004 : 62). However, there are multiple reasons for Standard English to become the dominant form of communication whenever Japanese and Westerners met. As one reason, Stanlaw (2004 : 63) quotes a commentary by an adjutant of Commodore Perry, Lt. George Preble:

> "They have a great aptitude at catching English sounds and ask the American name of everything they see, and so pick up a vocabulary of our language. They generally give us the Japanese, but it sounds so barbarous to our ears, we are not at much trouble to remember it."

The aforementioned passage is also known as 'Preble's Law' and outlines an attitude that became prevalent. English was the preferred way to communicate, since Westerners were unable (and mostly unwilling) to acquire the Japanese language – and the Japanese generally agreed with that, showing a condescending attitude towards most of the Westerners trying to master Japanese. This Japanese view is neatly summarized by influential linguist Suzuki Takao in 1978 (Stanlaw, 2004 : 268):

"Why teach Japanese to foreigners? ...
There is no reason to expect them to understand Japanese."

Another reason for the preference of English in international communication can be seen in the Japanese attitude towards their own language. Not only did they deem it too complicated for foreigners to learn, they even considered abolishing their 'bulky' native tongue themselves, to adopt English instead. Japan's first minister of education, Mori Arinori, lamented not only that Japanese would never be useful outside the country but also criticized the insufficient writing system which was still based on Chinese characters and therefore impossible to use as a phonetic transcription of the language (Stanlaw, 2004 : 65). In the end, the abolishment of Japanese never took place, but the mere *idea* of abolishing one's native tongue in favour of the language of a complete stranger (in cultural aspects) shows again the unique openness of the Japanese culture.

Still, the problem of the insufficient writing system had to be tackled. Of course, usage of Roman characters to transcribe Japanese was suggested very early since it would have eased communication with Westerners, but the popularity of Chinese characters in literary texts (since they can convey word meaning on multiple levels) and in other aspects of Japanese culture made this impossible (Stanlaw, 2004 : 64). According to Coulmas (1989 : 124-133), Chinese characters, *kanji*, had various downsides. Words that were being adapted from Chinese were naturally written as *kanji* and pronounced close to their Chinese origin; this filtered-through-Japanese-phonology adaptation of Chinese being called Sino-Japanese. But, later on, many of the *kanji* were also connected with the native Japanese pronunciation. This way, most *kanji* acquired both a Sino-Japanese and a native Japanse reading, the so-called *on-yomi* and *kun-yomi*. Even worse, some *kanji* acquired multiple *on-yomi* over the centuries of literal borrowing, since the meaning of a *kanji* might have changed in Chinese over time, resulting in all the possible meanings of a *kanji* accumulating in multiple *on-yomi*. This led to *kanji* with more than twenty possible meanings, which might be a poet's dream, but is quite the opposite for a learner of Japanese, native or not. Altogether, literacy was a skill difficult to acquire in Japan before the *Meiji*-Reforms. Instead of adapting the Roman alphabet, the solution was found by establishing the simplified *kana* syllabary (which had been available for centuries, but rarely used) as the official method for phonological transcription, together with limiting the set of Chinese characters to be used in written communication alongside the syllabary. This made learning written Japanese much easier, since a phonetic transcription of every Japanese word is now possible through *kana* and the number of *kanji* is limited to 1,950 items which are taught during school education – with that kind of *kanji*-knowledge, it is possible to read an average Japanese newspaper today. Nowadays, if a *kanji* is used that does not belong to the 1,950 default items, most newspapers or other print media add *furigana*, a tiny *kana* transcription, to the *kanji* symbol. Still, most Japanese have to continue reviewing the 'basic' set of *kanji* for the whole of their lives, and most *kanji* textbooks declare that forgetting the occasional *kanji* should be expected (Doitsu Center Ltd, 2006 : 19).

During the *Taisho* Period (1912-1926, following emperor Meiji's death in 1912), Japanese-English language contact rose to its first climax, with 63 percent of all borrowings present at the time having originated from English. The prestigious value of English was maintained "and studying it had immediate practical applications" (Stanlaw, 2004 : 68). Japan flourished, and as an ally of England mostly profited from WWI by obtaining former German areas in China while expanding their influence on the international markets (Dettmer, 1973 : 126). Many loans from the 1920s persist until today, one of them the *sarariman* from the initial example and, notably, many combinations with the word *gaaru* (*girl*), such as *mo-ga* (short for *modern girl*), *depaato-gaaru* (*department-store girl*), *gasorin-gaaru* (*gasoline-girl*) and the *ofisu gaaru* (*office girl*), reflecting the rising importance of women as a part of the reformed nation's workforce and, on the linguistic side, creating evidence for the Japanese tendency to clad new concepts in foreign words to ease transition. The term *ofisu gaaru* survived until today in *oo-eru*, which originates from the abbreviation *OL*, which is short for *office lady* (Stanlaw, 2004 : 69) – another example of the typical modifications English loanwords often undergo. Another factor was that linguistics became a vivid field of studies during Taisho period and scholars were well aware of the possible future influences of English on the Japanese language. Stanlaw (2004 : 69) quotes the most influential linguist of pre-war time, Ichikawa Sanki:

> "The influence of foreign languages – especially English – on Japanese is of such importance that probably not only words and expressions will continue to be borrowed in greater numbers but even the structure and grammar of the Japanese language will be considerably modified."

The nationalist military regimes during WWII tried to purge Western influences from Japanese culture – and with that, also from the language. The 'enemy's language' was no longer taught to the former extent at school (lowering a whole generation's ESL education) and English literature departments were closed at various universities (Ike, 1995 : 6). Also, there were efforts to replace English loans with terms of Japanese origin (Stanlaw, 2004 : 69). However, these replacements tended to sound rather strange to the 'modern' Japanese ear: words like *onban* (*euphonic board*) replacing the already very common *rekoodo* (*record*) or the *hoosoo-in* (*broadcast person*) taking the place of the *anaunsaa* (*announcer*) had an archaic or almost esoteric ring to them (Stanlaw, 2004 : 69). Anyway, the government's efforts proved to be futile and were quickly forgotten right after the war.

2.4 Bamboo English

After 1945, "the Japanese educational system was restructured" (Ike, 1995 : 6) and once again featured a thorough curriculum of English language studies. Still, the almost-abolished status of ESL during WW2 led to a lack of English competence of the contemporary generation of young adults. This led to problems since Japan was now occupied by American forces who hired large numbers of Japanese workers to maintain their facilities. Although formal English education, also for adults, was quickly re-established, "the occupation [...] provided a rich context for less formal linguistic contact" (Stanlaw, 2004 : 70) in the work-related communi-cation between the Japanese and the Americans. Another pidgin language evolved, so-called *Bamboo English*. The term actually incorporates a number of specialized sub-languages, since different varieties were spoken in various areas of everyday life as well as in different parts of East and Southeast Asia. In Japan, Stanlaw (2004 : 70) describes, at least two major varieties of Bamboo English were present – one was mostly used in a context of work at the U.S. bases, the other one (dubbed *pangurisshu*, literally meaning *street-walker English*) had the very spe-cialized purpose of providing a means of communication between the American soldiers and their various female acquaintances. Outside Japan, varieties of Bamboo English spread out thanks to the enormous number of American soldiers passing through Japan before starting service in the Korean War, who applied the pidgin heard in Japanese bases to their new envi-ronment as well – thus, the Korean variety of Bamboo English "was almost identical with that spoken in Japan, with only a few local Korean additions" (Stanlaw, 2004 : 70).

All the varieties had in common that they were dominated by English structures. Whereas during the times of the Yokohama Dialect, Japanese was the dominant partner in the commu-nication process with its new guests, now the Americans, as occupiers, were in the stronger position, and imposed a pidginized version of English on those unwilling to learn the standard language. "Word order and basic structure derived from English, though both American and Japanese speakers were somewhat indeterminate about this" (Stanlaw, 1987 : 97) and inter-changed possible options according to their liking. Besides that, the common simplifications of pidgin languages were visible. Temporal distinctions were only made through time markers,

16

a very simplified syntax was utilized and semantic extension played a role again, as can be seen in the following examples form Stanlaw (1987 : 97), Japanese items are highlighted and translated.

1. We're coming more *sukoshii* [little]
   We'll be there shortly.
2. Pail-u *sayoonara* [good-bye] it!
   Throw it away in the pail.
3. You all time speak work work. Sometime I think you butterfly.
   You always say you're out working. I sometimes think you're out playing around.
4. I beauty *saron* [salon] go, make nice, *deshoo* [probably; right]?
   Don't you think I should get a nice hairstyle at the beauty shop?

Stylistics and honorifics were strongly influenced by female Japanese, which "is characterized by the more extensive use of polite forms, honorific pronouns, and emphatics, interjections, and sentence-final particles" (Stanlaw, 1987 : 97). Most probably, the Americans using this kind of language learned it from their Japanese lady-friends or wives, which therefore were amusingly dubbed *ne-jibi* (*sleeping dictionaries*).

2.5 Post-war rising

The post-war period marked the beginning of the landslide-amounts of English loans assimi-lated into Japanese which has been going on until the present day. Formal education was re-formed multiple times, most notably changed by the influence of Harold E. Palmers Oral Method, which placed "greater emphasis on oral comprehension and speaking rather than reading and writing" (Koike, et al., 1995 : 17). Quickly, all pidgins became obsolete, and were slowly replaced by a Japanese variety of English developing out of the various efforts to ac-quire the language of the West. At the same time, the incorporation of loanwords became a more and more natural process and "today, it is impossible to interact in Japanese, or with Japanese, without recourse to English of one variety or another" (Stanlaw, 2004 : 73). This chapter will conclude with an illustration by Stanlaw (1987 : 102), showing how the three lines of language contact (pidginization, borrowing and formal education) are related to each other and their historical developments. Note that borrowing continued throughout the whole timeline, which is why the processes of borrowing will be examined in more detail in chapter four.

Figure 1 - Three lines of language contact

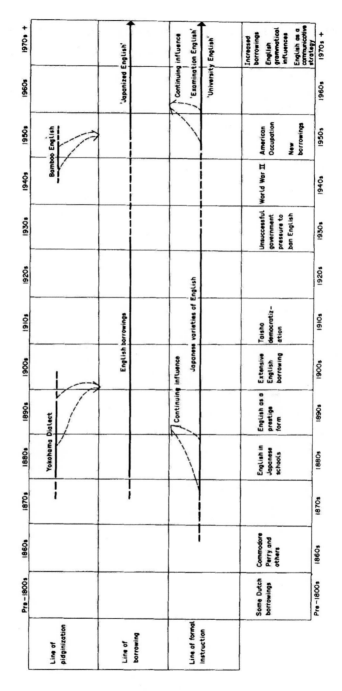

	Pre-1800s	1860s	1870s	1880s	1890s	1900s	1910s	1920s	1930s	1940s	1950s	1960s	1970s +
Line of pidginization			Yokohama Dialect								Bamboo English		'Japanized English'
Line of borrowing						English borrowings		Japanese varieties of English					
Line of formal instruction					Continuing influence							Continuing influence 'Examination English' 'University English'	
	Some Dutch borrowings	Commodore Perry and others		English in Japanese schools	English as a prestige form	Extensive English borrowing	Taisho democratiz- ation		Unsuccessful government pressure to ban English	World War II	American Occupation New borrowings		Increased borrowings English grammatical influences English as a communicative strategy
	Pre-1800s	1860s	1870s	1880s	1890s	1900s	1910s	1920s	1930s	1940s	1950s	1960s	1970s +

18

3. The contemporary status of English in Japan

Chapter 2 showed that in the past, English was often regarded as the superior language and the Japanese were eager to learn it. They hoped that it would help to modernize their hopelessly derelict country, propelling it into the same 'league' as all the Western nations. Clearly, English did indeed play an important role, establishing itself as 'the language of the West' as it was spoken by the dominant forces. However, the worshipping of English and the Western culture quickly passed its climax as the Japanese realized that they were no longer lagging behind – resulting in the rise of nationalism mostly during WW2. This new pride of the Japanese identity was only diminished for a short period of time during the American occupation and has nowadays reached a level of healthy self-confidence, mostly due to the well-known economic success of Japan during the past decades. Japanese as a language has a right to exist, and more Westerners than ever are learning it to improve their contacts with one of the leading economical powers of the world (Stanlaw, 2004 : 272). But even though the Japanese now see their own language as equal (or sometimes superior) to Western languages, the importance of English has not declined, but rather increased and shifted in focus, mostly due to the economic power of Japan being rooted in international commerce.

In this chapter, the current status of English in Japan will be examined from multiple perspectives. After a quick examination of the current relationship of Japan with the West, this chapter will continue with an illustration of how much importance English has for the Japanese population both from a nationwide perspective, concerning international economic relations, and an individual perspective, showing how English is a major requirement for many Japanese to be successful in life. Following this, the characteristics of Japanese ESL and its developments since its emergence during the Meiji-Restoration will be analyzed. Also there will be a discussion as to why English education faced a number of problems in Japan – some of them still persisting today even after multiple reforms. The chapter will be concluded with examples for the presence of English in Japanese media, such as advertisements and items from popular culture.

3.1 Relations with the outside

Politically, contemporary Japan is not much different from most Western nations. After the war, parties and trade unions acquired an importance similar to the West, and Japan wove close relations with the U.S. and their befriended nations, culminating in Japan's inclusion in the UNO in 1956 (Dettmer, 1973 : 134-135). Relations with other Asian countries were less easy to maintain, for example the political situation concerning South Korea could only be "normalized on the basis of large financial payments by Japan [in 1965], and not until 1972 [...] Japan established full diplomatic relations with Peking" (Reischauer, 1977 : 113). Besides a political crisis in 1960 concerning a new Security Treaty with the U.S. and some tensions due to the American position in the Vietnam War, the situation was much like in any other nation. "Student unrest, which was at its height around 1968 in Japan as elsewhere in the world, contributed to the political turmoil" (Reischauer, 1977 : 114), but quickly subsided alongside the foreign policy crisis as the Americans began to withdraw from Vietnam. Meanwhile, the so-called "economic wonder" (Reischauer, 1977 : 115) propelled Japan into the higher circles of world economy, making it the third largest economic unit worldwide by the end of the 1960s. Arts, both Western and Japanese, were flourishing and education levels were very high, with about 90 percent of the students completing high school – probably a world record and an indicator for general public prosperity (Reischauer, 1977 : 117). Japan took over its role as a leading global player in mere decades and maintained this status until today.

It has been shown that, economically and politically, Japan has developed a clearly international attitude. Truly, as a visitor, a foreigner will always be treated with utmost politeness and deference, but beneath this outer layer the Japanese cherish a strong separateness, often without realizing themselves. Diplomat and scholar Edwin Oldfather Reischauer, author of one of the most influential works on Japanese Studies ("The Japanese"), points out: "They appear to have a greater feeling of group solidarity and a correspondingly stronger sense of their difference from others" (Reischauer, 1977 : 401). Reischauer sees these attitudes as a result of multiple factors that actually do make the Japanese quite different, especially the distinctive language, the history of isolation and its unique role in modern economy. Together with a traditionally very definite distinction between being inside and outside of a group, the Japanese have developed a strong awareness of being different from the rest of the world – not necessarily superior, but different. Most Japanese would react affronted if they were accused of nationalism, and they would be right, since Japan is, as mentioned, very internationally oriented indeed. This is reflected not only in thorough international coverage in the media but also in the educational system which, beside the foreign language curriculum, puts great efforts in various international cultural studies. The coverage of Eastern countries in Western schools pales in comparison to the manifold lessons on Western culture available in basic Japanese education (Reischauer, 1977 : 402).

If the Japanese attitude were to be called nationalism, it would, again, be a special kind. The Japanese' connection to their country is totally unlike classical notions of patriotism: especially immediately after the war, the Japanese started to avoid all notions of nationalism (even the word itself) and adopted an international attitude. The Japanese national anthem for example is known to many children only as the *sumou* song, since they only know it from TV-broadcasts of sumo wrestling bouts, where it is played before the fight begins (Reischauer, 1977 : 403). This shows that Japanese do not need such outer representations of patriotism, since they are permanently aware of their belonging to the Japanese nation, or rather: the Japanese 'group'. As Reischauer puts it, "the first answer of a Japanese to the question 'Who are you?' is likely to be 'A Japanese.'" (1977 : 403). Of course, the author's observations are based mostly on personal experiences (as he admits himself) and the attitude has surely been weakened over the past decades of globalization. Nevertheless, this mental seclusion of the Japanese people from the rest of humanity is still present in many aspects of life and most non-Japanese residents of Japan will probably agree that integration into the Japanese community is still not easy. Concerning the topic of this paper, this innate separateness is considered a way to explain the seeming paradox between the openness of the Japanese both culturally and linguistically and the simultaneous refusal to let foreigners into their inner circle – an inner circle as large as Japan itself.

3.2 A need for (better) English

In my review of Japanese language-related history in chapter 1 it was highlighted that English was deemed very important for the long-time-isolated, politically derelict country to catch up with Western nations. Obviously, the Japanese *did* catch up, as can be seen in their economical importance in the world. The Japanese language, though very saturated with foreign loans, is no longer deemed unsatisfactory or too complicated, and the idea to abolish it has long been forgotten. Still, the popularity of English is more present than ever, as is visible in its role in the education system and its prevalence in the media. What makes the English language retain its popularity in contemporary Japan?

One reason is the very international character of the Japanese economy, which relies heavily on import and export of goods. Therefore, "for many Japanese, their interest in English is mo-

21

tivated by very practical concerns. [...] They study English in order to pass university entrance exams, to meet the needs of their present jobs, or to improve their qualifications so that they can get a better job in the future" (Morrow, 1995 : 87). The traditional use of English for international communication has persisted in Japan, since the educational infrastructure for learning English is well-established while the Western educational system is very focused on the Romance languages and Japanese is rarely taught in basic education. Still, the level of English proficiency obtained in school and high school (and often university as well) does usually not suffice to enable the learners to communicate about work-related topics; thus "among adult learners, work-related reasons are the primary ones" (Morrow, 1995 : 87) to study English. Of course, there are many self-study materials available, but there is the question whether this kind of material can provide the *kind* of English necessary for business purposes. There might be general 'Business English' courses, but there are more efficient ways of language training. The basic question is: If a learner needs English only for specific purposes in specific fields, what kind of English should he learn? And, furthermore, are grammar and vocabulary all that is needed for successful communication?

There is a stereotype that while an American usually starts a speech with a joke, a Japanese speaker would much more likely start with an apology (Nishiyama, 1995 : 31). Though extreme, the stereotype has a true core and hints at the various pitfalls in intercultural communication, for which Japanese students of English are not sufficiently prepared. There is an enormous difference in style between Japanese and English which cannot be covered by learning grammar and vocabulary, on which standard ESL in Japan focuses. Efficient communication "requires familiarity with the communication behaviour of the speakers of the majority language, their social mores, values and some degree of creative expression" (Nishiyama, 1995 : 27). Fluent Japanese speakers of English, however skilful their mastery of the language is, often "find themselves being accused of beating around the bush" (Nishiyama, 1995 : 29), since the Japanese tendency to communicate more indirectly does not translate well into most Western environments, especially the very direct world of American businessmen. Still, it is only natural for Japanese patterns to influence a second language, especially if those patterns are strongly connected to the cultural background of the speaker. One has to keep in mind that harmony and politeness are important factors in everyday Japanese life which were established centuries ago. In a densely populated country like Japan, it was vitally important for everyone to 'get along' nicely, if just for the sake of survival (Nishiyama, 1995 :

30). The Japanese language therefore incorporated various methods of establishing and maintaining harmonious relationships between speakers. Besides innumerable pat phrases, there are different verb forms used to indicate different levels of politeness, often depending on the status in the vertically organized Japanese social hierarchy. The Japanese language knows various stages of politeness and deference, but in contemporary Japan the variety has been reduced a little. Most foreign learners of Japanese will now learn the *masu* form, a kind of standard-politeness, which will most probably not insult anyone at least by grammar alone. The Japanese themselves however have much trouble applying their complex system of verbal politeness to English, resulting in the before mentioned "beating around the bush" (Nishiyama, 1995 : 29). As Nishiyama puts it, "in Japanese there are various ways of saying 'No' without using the word" (1995 : 30), mostly through explaining the reasons for a refusal instead of stating it outright. This can be highly irritating to Westerners, who just want a clear answer. Besides these problems rooted in cultural heritage there are much more obvious difficulties concerning the interpretation of metaphors and other misunderstandings of a similar kind. Therefore it becomes clear that a Japanese learner of English who needs to intensively communicate with native speakers of English on Business trips or similar occasions will have to do much more training than just memorizing a grammar and a phrasebook.

In 1993, Phillip R. Morrow conducted research on the language training programme of a big Japanese company: Toshiba, well-known producer of home-electronics. According to his paper on his findings (Morrow, 1995 : 90-92), about 500 employees enrol for English language training programmes offered by the 'Toshiba International Training Center' (ITC) each year, and there are always more applications than actual seats in the seminars. Unlike the English taught in schools which is strongly biased towards the so-called "translation method" (Koike, et al., 1995 : 24) and therefore more focused on grammar and written communication, the seminars offered by the ITC emphasize the more direct communicative skills of speaking and listening. This corresponds with the felt needs of the learners, who indicated that they are weakest at speaking and listening comprehension (58% and 34% of participants, respectively) when asked about their weaknesses by Morrow (1995 : 95). To fill this gap, the ITC offers a very diverse curriculum. Starting from 'General English' courses, which are offered at five different levels and are taught to rather heterogeneous groups of employees, the ITC then offers various courses and curricula for the specific needs of certain groups of employees. 'Business English for Technicians' focuses on technical English for employees who might have to write English manuals for new products and need to communicate effectively with other technicians on offshore facilities. A similar programme is offered for managing personnel, the 'International Businesspersons' Class'. In these courses, employees who are designated to obtain management positions in foreign facilities are trained for exactly this purpose and probably most thoroughly, since two or three months of further language study abroad are mandatory. The course is usually followed by an immediate dispatching of the 'specialists' to work or to conduct research abroad. Additionally, the ITC offers courses in presentation, telephone usage, technical writing, negotiating and cross-cultural business studies, thus completing the list of purposes for which employees might need to improve their English.

All the courses offered by the ITC have three things in common: small class size, intensive specialized format and a high level of motivation among the students. The curriculum is tailored as closely to the future needs of the participants as possible, including considerations like the additional usage of audio material from Asian speakers of English (Morrow, 1995 : 94), to prepare the students for the very likely encounters with other Asian varieties of English. Furthermore, "the emphasis on cross-cultural communication in all of these courses reflects a perception on the part of Toshiba's management that communication problems often result from cultural differences rather than lack of knowledge about language" (Morrow, 1995 : 96). As already mentioned, the ITC tries to fill the gap in the Japanese approach to English language teaching – a gap left by schools who tailor their courses towards the so-called 'Exam English', a variety of English fit for the entrance exams to universities (Koike, et al., 1995 : 17-18). While this of course helps students to enrol in a university, it has downsides for students who decide to enter business life immediately after high school. The fault may lie with the universities, who have stuck to their practice of testing English skills in a highly 'grammatical' way, with little interest in more communicative approaches. Anyway, there appear to be some problems and contradictions in the Japanese way of learning (and teaching) English, which will be reviewed in more detail in section 3.3.

3.3 Japanese ESL

For most Europeans, or people who speak an Indo-European language, learning English is comparably easy thanks to the common linguistically genetic background. Leaving behind the Eastern borders of the 'old world', things grow more difficult with every mile. I myself acquired some basic knowledge of Japanese in an introductory course at the University of Siegen, and the fact that this very, very basic course lasted for three consecutive semesters shows that learning Japanese is something quite different from learning an Indo-European language. Without an intensive course format as offered for those enrolled in Japanese Studies, or at least a very high level of enthusiasm while continuing training at home, it is near to impossible to acquire a level of Japanese that could at least be described as 'useful'. Personally, I did not have much time to keep my Japanese 'in shape', and so I am quite happy about the fact that my knowledge about Japanese grammar and other basic linguistic features is still sufficient for me to confidently review the sources I needed while conducting research for this thesis. Any kind of effective communication with a Japanese person in his or her native tongue, however, would require some thorough reviewing of vocabulary and phrases on my part first (not to mention the writing), since the exotic shape of Japanese words, both written and audible, is quite easily forgotten. I am sharing these personal experiences because in my opinion, they mirror what a Japanese learner of English might experience during his studies. English is so utterly *foreign* to the Japanese learner, even though he may know a large number of English terms from loans and, in more recent years, the media. However, this kind of 'vocabulary' has not much to do with actual English (as will be discussed in chapter four) and does not help with grammar, anyway. The Japanese government tried to overcome the obstacles with a very thorough programme of English education which was established early on in the reformed Japan.

As was already shown in this thesis, English was introduced as a mandatory subject after the *Meiji* reforms, when it was considered a must in order to push forward the country. But as soon as the 1920s, objections to this thorough coverage of all educational institutions with ESL arose, since "most of the students [would] not use English in daily life, and so trying to master it [would be] a great waste of time and effort on their part" (Tanaka, et al., 1995 : 123). On the other side, there was awareness of the insufficiency of English teaching concerning communicative purposes. As early as 1922, Harold E. Palmer, a lecturer from London who had been invited to Japan to establish an Institute for Research in English Teaching, created a so-called "'Oral Method' based on his understanding of how babies began to master their mother tongue" (Koike, et al., 1995 : 117). His innovations had to wait quite some time before being implemented, due to WWII, where teaching English was at an all-time low. Reforms shortly after the war, though, quickly revealed Palmer's influence, since "greater emphasis on oral comprehension and speaking rather than reading and writing was apparent" (Koike, et al., 1995 : 17) and later, the audio-lingual approach to teaching English became more widespread.

25

Still, it was hard for senior high schools to implement the new approaches, since the universities stuck with their focus on grammar and written English in their entrance exams (Koike, et al., 1995 : 18). Arguments about how and why to teach English persisted throughout modern Japanese history, alternating between reducing the importance of English in the curriculum and the improvement of ESL to be more efficient (Tanaka, et al., 1995 : 122-123). One great controversy arose in 1974 due to a public "debate between Hiraizumi, a member of the House of Councillors, and Watanabe, Professor of (English) Linguistics at Sophia University" (Tanaka, et al., 1995 : 123). Among other issues, Hiraizumi claimed that while English is a mandatory subject in high schools since it is thoroughly tested in university entrance exams, "English (or any foreign language) education in Japan is totally ineffective, for most graduates can hardly speak, read, write, or understand the language which they 'have presumably learned'" (Tanaka, et al., 1995 : 123). The reasons for this are that students are not well motivated because English plays virtually no role in their daily lives and they only learn it to pass entrance exams with requirements that are too high, while the teaching itself suffers from problems arising from the structural differences between Japanese and English. Hiraizumi therefore proposed to consider whether mandatory ESL courses make any sense at all and whether English should be an elective subject besides other languages, and also how the ESL teaching could be more effective in the compact format of an intensive course. Additionally, he proposed to remove English from university exams, where it is currently mandatory for all courses of study, whether they actively incorporate English in their curriculum or not (Tanaka, et al., 1995 : 124). Many of Hiraizumi's claims are still valid today, such as the lack of practical communicative competence and the problem of 'Exam English'. But so are the counterarguments of Watanabe, which are as follows: He claims that while "Japanese people are not good at speaking English, [...] speaking is a different skill from other skills, such as comprehension, writing, and the knowledge of grammar, so that being unable to speak English does not necessarily mean that teaching English is useless altogether" (Tanaka, et al., 1995 : 124), even though it is evidently difficult for students to acquire fluent English. But based on exactly this problem, he defends the testing of English as part of university entrance exams. He considers the skill of English (even if it is mostly written communication) a good means to "measure students' intellectual standard because the knowledge of English is acquired only after diligent and concentrated efforts" (Tanaka, et al., 1995 : 124). Furthermore, Watanabe objects to making English an elective subject, since the learners might have opportunities to improve their skills later in life. However, this would only be possible with the "potential" given to students during school, even though the results of this education might not lead to mastery of communicative abilities by themselves. Depriving a part of the students of this potential might lead to a kind of elitism among those who are 'allowed' to learn English, says Watanabe.

In the end, Hiraizumis proposals could not be implemented for various reasons, the most obvious being that if students were to have enough training to sufficiently master English, they would not have enough time to work on other subjects. Nevertheless, the public debate of Hiraizumi and Watanabe led to more awareness of the problems with Japanese ESL and forced the Ministry of Education to deal with the matter (Tanaka, et al., 1995 : 124). This resulted in major revisions of (English) language instruction at both high school and university level. Most notably, "the Course of Study revised in March 1989 puts more emphasis on the communication ability of high school students" (Tanaka, et al., 1995 : 125) to move away from the prevalent translation-based method of teaching English. The most visible modification of the curriculum to put these revisions into action is the addition of 'Oral Communication' courses with emphasis on listening and speaking. Additionally, an increasing number of native speakers of English entered Japan through the Japanese Education and Teaching (JET) program, which started in 1987 with 848 people (Tanaka, et al., 1995 : 125) and has been very successful since. "In 2009, the Programme has welcomed 4,682 participants from 38 countries" (JET-Programme, 2009). Most of these native speakers are hired as so-called 'Assistant Language Teachers' (ALTs) or, more specifically for our case, 'Assistant English Teachers' (AETs) to support Japanese teachers and to add a source of original English to classes – for some students living in more rural areas the AETs are the only way of ever meeting a native speaker of English, which makes the JET participants an invaluable addition to the ESL system of Japan (Koike, et al., 1995 : 20).

The problem of 'utter foreignness' when Japanese students are confronted with English has already been mentioned. Another way to tackle this problem is to already present English to younger children – this way, they can much easier adapt to pronunciation and rhythm of the foreign language, as children can adapt easier to new speech patterns. Teaching English at primary schools was therefore an unavoidable proposal and in 1987, as much as 103 private primary schools were teaching English regularly. However, the number was less than 1 percent of all primary schools in Japan (Koike, et al., 1995 : 22) and even though the Ministry is now encouraging the teaching of English in all private and public schools, this is not yet man-

27

datory and the contents of the curriculum are only vaguely outlined in the official guidelines (Graham, 2009). This fact results in a problem for middle school teachers. If the middle school has multiple private and public elementary schools in the neighbourhood, teachers are often confronted with very heterogeneous classes when it comes to the already available level of English proficiency among the students. Even though most elementary schools only teach some rudimentary elements of English to the children, usually through songs, and aim for their ability to introduce themselves and ask basic questions, this makes a huge difference when these children are now seated next to children who had less (or different) English lessons during primary school or maybe had no contact to English altogether. The only proper way to deal with this is by splitting up the class according to the available level of English (Tanaka, et al., 1995 : 127), but since this is not always possible there might be hardships for those who had no preparation in English or, vice versa, the children with some English background might not be sufficiently challenged by the curriculum.

The Japanese government has shown a great willingness to reform the methods of teaching English over the past decades, since they recognized that "TEFL has become a big social issue" and "[they tend] to relate [...] their political, economic, administrative and educational policies whenever they are relevant to each other" (Koike, et al., 1995 : 24). The way English is learned by the Japanese is influenced by multiple factors, such as Japanese social psychology, the hierarchically structured society and specific Japanese language structures as well as communication strategies and the prevailing translation-based method of learning English which (still) is the best preparation for the mostly writing-focused university entrance exams (Koike, et al., 1995 : 23-24). All this must be taken into account to constantly revise the ESL program of Japan, and it happens just this way. But in spite of all the efforts to introduce the English language as thoroughly as possible, even against the occasional cry against the menacing "hegemony of English" (Tanaka, et al., 1995 : 128), one very basic problem remains and is unlikely to change soon. Japanese ESL is for the most part not English as a Second Language, but more appropriately described as Japanese EFL – English as a Foreign Language.

3.4 English in arts and ads

As a contrast to the apparent problems with English education, the paradoxically opposite role of English in modern cultural items in Japan will be presented. In the past decades, one of the major sources of English available to the Japanese youth has come in the form of various me-

28

dia products, especially through pop-culture and advertisement. Concerning pop-culture, it has been mentioned in the introduction that the Japanese top 40 are more often than they are not completely comprised of titles with some relation to English, revealing the popularity of the language for Japan's youth. However, this popularity is not restricted to imported native English titles but appears to extend to virtually any kind of usage of English in songs from native Japanese artists as well. Contemporary songs that are part of modern Japanese pop-culture are usually referred to as *J-Pop*, and a very typical characteristic of this genre is the heavy use of both English loans and plain English as an integral part of the lyrics. As an example, a passage from *'Cagayake! GIRLS'* has been selected. It is actually the opening theme of the Japanese anime TV series *K-On!*, which has been very successful this year, spawning various commercially successful spin-off media products. The series revolves around a group of high school girls who form a rock band, comically struggling with all the problems they encounter on their endeavours. The song is prototypical for J-Pop and the intermedial connections it often has to other media products[3] and it is also a good example for the usage of English in contemporary J-Pop.

Original lyrics	Romanized version	Translation
Jumping Now ガチでウルワシ Never Ending Girls' Life	Jumping Now GACHI de URUWASHI Never Ending Girls' Life	Jumping Now Serious and pretty Never Ending Girls' Life
日々マジ ライブだし待ったなし 早起きしても早寝は Non Non Non!	hibi MAJI RAIBU dashi matta nashi hayaoki shite mo hayane wa Non Non Non!	The days are truly live and have no waiting Even if I wake up early, going to bed early is Non Non Non!
目一杯Shouting ワッショイ ガチでスバラシ Never Ending Girls' Song	meippai Shouting WASSHOI GACHI de SUBARASHI Never Ending Girls' Song	With my best, I'm Shouting loudly Serious and wonderful Never Ending Girls' Song
午後ティータイムには持ってこい 片想いでも玉砕で Here We Go!	gogo TIITAIMU ni wa motte koi kataomoi demo gyokusai de Here We Go!	Afternoon teatime is just the thing for me. Even if it's unrequited love or a sound defeat, Here We Go!
歌えば Shining After School	utaeba Shining After School	When we sing, we're Shining After School

Table 1 – Cagayake! GIRLS

---

[3] Anime, Japanese animated films and series, are often strongly intertwined with J-Pop and J-Rock music, since it is quite usual that opening and ending themes are produced by contemporary artists, this way either promoting the artist's work or, vice versa, making the anime more interesting for fans of the artist. A lot of times, songs are produced entirely for the anime industry in the first place and released only later as a single together with the first airing of the anime. Another variant would be that one of the anime's *seiyuus*, a voice actor, starts a secondary career as a singer by providing the opening theme for the show he or she is actually starring in. This way, the anime and the music industry, both economical behemoths themselves, create an even bigger commercial 'success-machinery' by profiting from each other's momentum.

Table 1 shows the song's chorus in three different ways. First, there is the original Japanese transcription in *kana* and *kanji* signs, together with the English passages printed in roman letters – this is the way the lyrics would be printed, for example, on a leaflet shipped with the CD. The next version shows the same text in *romaji*, and the author has kindly highlighted loanwords by capitalizing them. In the original version, loans can be distinguished from 'normal' Japanese as they are written in *katakana* rather than *hiragana* (*katakana* are made out of mostly straight lines and generally look more 'edgy' than the *hiragana*, which have smoother shapes). This way of indication is very useful to the Japanese reader since it makes a quick distinction easier, allowing a change in pronunciation and tone if necessary. The third version of the lyrics is a translation made by a fan of the series and thus does not originate from a professional source, which is why errors may be possible. Still, the translation is sufficient to get an impression of the content. Line breaks and spaces have been added by the author to improve overall clarity and to make the association between the different segments more obvious.

If the Romanized version is taken as a reference, the passage consists of 50 words. Out of this 50, 19 are made up by the English passages, and a further 8 words can be classified as loans. Thus, a total of 27 words (54 %) are apparently not of Japanese origin. The remaining parts of the song have a little less prominent presence of English, but follow the principle established in the chorus. Even allowing the possible intention of the artist to go a little overboard on English to create a parody of typical English-infused J-Pop (which would fit the series' topic), the percentage still shows how important the usage of English is in contemporary pop culture. According to Stanlaw, English is mostly used for eight different purposes in Japanese pop music (Stanlaw, 2004 : 104):

i.   English as an 'audacious' device
ii. English as a 'symbolic' device
iii. English as a 'poetic' device
iv. English as an 'exotic' device
v.   English as a means of creating 'new structural forms'
vi. English as a means of 'relexifying' and 're-exoticizing' the Japanese language
vii. English to express aspects of modern Japanese consumer culture
viii. English words as a means to express images of domestic life in modern Japan

Obviously, *Cagayake! GIRLS* is not the most poetic or symbolically deep song (unlike the multiple examples Stanlaw uses in his very thorough analysis), but there are still aspects from the above list that can be applied to '*Cagayake! GIRLS*' as well.

30

The overall context of the song[4] supports the fact that English has proven to be a favourite tool for female artists: they use it to put new, more feministic views into writing which would otherwise be much harder to convey using traditional Japanese. As I already mentioned in chapter 2, certain forms are mostly used by females and traditionally convey a comparably archaic feminine stance. According to Stanlaw (2004 : 131), Japanese women originally were a minority when it came to written communication, since the Chinese *kanji* signs were traditionally only to be learned by men. While the male part of society could gain considerable prestige through mastering written Chinese, it was considered 'unladylike' for women to learn this language, which effectively not only led to an exclusion of the women from the male power structure but also deprived them of means to produce any kind of written output. Therefore it were the women who profited most from the introduction of the simplified *hiragana* syllabary, since it enabled them to transcribe spoken Japanese into a written from without having received tutoring in the complicated *kanji*. *Hiragana* and *katakana* could be learned quickly and did not touch the taboo of the 'unladylike' *kanji*. For similar reasons, the usage of English words, both in *romaji* or transcribed to the *katakana* syllabary, became a very useful component in female literature, with authors who used English equivalents of Japanese items to give them a new semantic value – much like the classical Japanese literature where the multiple meanings of *kanji* signs were utilized as an stylistic device.

This kind of usage of English reflects the idea of 'audacity' mentioned by Stanlaw and can be found to some extent in the usage of English phrases in '*Cagayake! GIRLS*' as well. Throughout the song, the English term *girl* is used instead of the various Japanese equivalents, thus differentiating the modern, powerful *girl* from the somewhat archaic role models conveyed by the Japanese forms used to refer to young women, such as *shojo* (*maiden*), *musume* (*daughter*) or the more modern *kanojo* (*girlfriend*). The song underlines this additionally by not even using the loan *gaaru* (girl) but instead the original English form itself, alluding to an international image of female emancipation. When it comes to the other reasons Stanlaw lists to use English in pop songs, it is used here to create new structural forms, in this case by alternating Japanese sentence segments with English ones. This creates something like a rhyme scheme (e.g. by paralleling '*Non Non Non!*' with '*Here We Go!*'), a technique "usually absent from Japanese verse" (Stanlaw, 2004 : 113). Another item to which a possible 'intention'

---

[4] The series is strongly influenced by some kind of 'girl-power' theme, as is already implied by the song's title which roughly translates to '*Shine! GIRLS*'.

from Stanlaw's list could be applied to is the word *tiitaimu* (*tea time*), since it could be seen as a description of the Western idea of a tea time (or afternoon tea), which would fit to no. viii (domestic images from modern Japan). It might also refer to the nowadays innumerable Western patisseries in Japan, which are particularly popular with women and have become a part of modern Japanese consumer culture (no. vii in Stanlaw's list). If one of the main themes of the series is considered, i.e. the girls' dream of international success as a rock band, English additionally becomes a symbol (ii) for Western success stories as well as a device to re-exoticize (vi) the 'boring' Japanese language by intermingling it with 'fresh and global' English.

Because an artist's usage of English is usually motivated by poetic intentions, it is thoroughly pondered upon and every syllable has its purpose – or at least, an artist can always claim that whatever he or she wrote was intended to be 'open for interpretation' all the same. Looking at the world of Japanese advertising, the priorities seem to be spread quite differently. English is *en vogue* in advertising as much as in any other country, but the Japanese openness towards linguistic assimilation sometimes leads to excessive use of English in a company's or shop's striving for internationalism. Sometimes, the observer might get the impression that English is used only for the sake of using it, without any apparent rational reason. While there are many attempts to translate something to English to make it accessible to foreigners, an equal or maybe even bigger number of examples shows English being used for the 'exotic and modern ring' the language has to the Japanese audience. This phenomenon provides the (English-speaking) globe with most amusing examples of the so-called *Engrish* (the term alludes to the cliché difficulties concerning the differentiation of 'L' and 'R'). Amusing examples can be found en masse on the internet, on websites such as *Engrish.com*, from which the following three examples have been taken:

Picture 1 - Examples for 'Engrish'

32

While some of the examples for comical *Engrish* relish in the poor grammar and vocabulary issues apparent in some valiant translator's work (as can be seen in the first image in picture 1), most examples come from advertisement and public relations, ranging from slogans (image 2) over packaging and brand names to a more graphical usage, as for example on clothing (image 3). One of the primary reasons for using English in advertisement is the greater graphical flexibility when using Roman letters, since the *kana* as well as *kanji* signs are much harder to morph into visually more interesting (and still readable) fonts than the much simpler shapes of *romaji*. Usage of Roman letters enables advertisers to make their product stand out, even if the English words are mostly never read or understood, making additional information in Japanese script necessary. Similarly, the use of English slogans stands out against the over-used Japanese ones – an invaluable aid for advertisers in an economy where hundreds of new products are introduced to customers all the time. The customers seeing an advert are usually not fluent speakers of English, with a vocabulary originating from loans and, more often than not, other adverts. Advertisers therefore frequently use incorrect grammar to convey an abstract meaning implied by the separate words, as can be seen in image 2 where the adjective *happy* is used as a noun, probably due to the fact that the word *happy* is more known than *happiness*, which would also require to use the more 'complicated' *some* instead of *a*. A study on borrowings in Japanese advertisements by Kyoko Takashi (1990 : 331) shows that most of the borrowings in the reviewed material are merely special-effects-givers (45.10%), or brand names (25.30%). Lexical-gap fillers and technical terms only contributed 15.90% and 13.30%, respectively. The bottom line is: if it works and gives off a good impression to the customer, correct grammar can be neglected – as well as comprehensibleness for proficient speakers of English. It has to be noted, of course, that the examples of *Engrish* known to the West are, in spite of their numbers, still the 'black sheep', since many companies put a lot more effort into their English slogans and product names, often consulting native speakers of English. However, probably very few customers will appreciate these efforts.

4. Loanwords: borrowed or made in Japan?

In the past chapters, an overview of the role of English for the Japanese culture in both past and present has been given. This thesis began, however, with an example of a Japanese sentence which was made up almost entirely out of words which are not of Japanese origin, specifically loanwords. This led to the question why the Japanese show such an enormous affinity to items from foreign languages, the English language in particular, while at the same time insisting on their separateness from other cultures. The past chapters have, besides establishing the historical background, mostly dealt with the role of Standard English in Japanese culture. This means the instances were (near) native English or ESL are important to the Japanese, and what reasons there are for its use – ranging from internationalization over usage as a new creative tool for poetry to the simple foreign 'ring' English words have in advertising. So far, there has been only a mere suggestion that there exists another major representation of English in Japan, namely through borrowings and nativized Japanese English. As mentioned in section 3.3 on Japanese ESL, most young Japanese who do not have contact to native speakers of English still have words of English origin in their mental vocabulary. These are not only taken from popular culture but everyday Japanese speech, which could not work nowadays without relying on English loans. Ever since the seclusion of the country from Western influences ended, items entered the Japanese language continually. The surge of borrowing reached landslide proportions after WW2, with more than half of the 25.000 loanwords known in 1980 entering the language (Kay, 1995 : 68). In contemporary Japan, the mass media help keeping up the flow of new vocabulary more than ever, reflecting the internationalization of the country.

Sections 4.1 to 4.3 will first outline the processes involved in borrowing and how the Japanese assimilate English words into their own language, using methods developed over the course of their language-contact history. This will be followed by a description of the reasons for borrowing and for using loans instead of original Japanese vocabulary in general, also touching upon the concept of *wa-sei eigo*, the so-called *English-made-in-Japan*.

4.1 The process of borrowing

A word may become part of another linguistic environment for various reasons, the plainest one being that it is used to describe a concept formerly unknown in the new environment. The German expression *Kindergarten* has found its way into the English vocabulary because of the fact that it was a unique approach to child care. Similar examples would be the names for different types of food like the French *baguette*, or expressions from various fields of science. However, there are two different states such a word can obtain in the new language: it is either a foreign word or a loanword. The difference is that when a word is considered a foreign word, it retains its status of being 'outside' the standard language, even though it may be used as regular as native expressions. The loanword, on the other hand, has been assimilated into the native language so much that its foreign roots are often no longer easily detectible; and even if they are, speakers would not bother much on a conscious level. In short, the foreign word has retained its 'foreignness' while the loanword has been nativized into the target language – quite often, the latter happens when a foreign word has been in use for years and speakers more or less 'forget' about the foreign origins of the term. What makes Japanese special here is that the number of foreign words that acquire loanword status is much higher than in many other languages, and the process of nativization appears to work much faster and, to some extent, differently.

While many foreign words retain most of their original pronunciation and morphology, loanwords often undergo changes on various levels to obtain a 'shape' closer to the standards of the target language in which they are embedded. With Japanese, this mostly happens by adapting the pronunciation of the original term for the constraints of the Japanese syllable-based system. Basically, the Japanese can utilize their domestic phonetic script that is available through the *kana* syllabaries to immediately transcribe any foreign term they hear; possibly even on a temporary basis (Kay, 1995 : 69), for example when trying to write down a foreigner's name. The ease of this process makes nativization much more likely than in other languages, where foreign words usually acquire a near-native shape only over years of deformation by hearsay. Or, as Kay puts it (1995 : 72), "there is no linguistic barrier to the absorption into Japanese of words from other languages".

Since the Japanese, like any other group, have difficulty reproducing all the sounds that might appear in a foreign word, most of these will undergo phonological change to accommodate the Japanese sound system (Kay, 1995 : 69). The system is based on syllables, which are reflected in the *kana* syllabaries, *hiragana* and *katakana*. The following table shows the basic syllables; the almost equal amount of variations that makes up the remaining syllabary is neglected here. The table shows the consonants (left) available for combination with the vowels (top). The fields contain the Romanization according to the Hepburn-system on the left, the *hiragana* transcription in the middle and the *katakana* on the right.

	a	あ ア	i	い イ	u	う ウ	e	え エ	o	お オ
k	ka	か カ	ki	き キ	ku	く ク	ke	け ケ	ko	こ コ
s	sa	さ サ	shi	し シ	su	す ス	se	せ セ	so	そ ソ
t	ta	た タ	chi	ち チ	tsu	つ ツ	te	て テ	to	と ト
n	na	な ナ	ni	に ニ	nu	ぬ ヌ	ne	ね ネ	no	の ノ
h	ha	は ハ	hi	ひ ヒ	fu	ふ フ	he	へ ヘ	ho	ほ ホ
m	ma	ま マ	mi	み ミ	mu	む ム	me	め メ	mo	も モ
y	ya	や ヤ	[i	い イ	yu	ゆ ユ	[e	え エ	yo	よ ヨ
r	ra	ら ラ	ri	り リ	ru	る ル	re	れ レ	ro	ろ ロ
w	wa	わ ワ	[i	い イ	[u	う ウ	[e	え エ	o	を ヲ
n, m	-	ん ン							©2002 Christian Rosenträter http://www.christianrosentraeter.de	

Table 2 - Excerpt from kana syllabaries

For the transcription of foreign words, solely *katakana* signs are used. Upon encountering a sound that is not available, one must choose the nearest Japanese equivalent. Other restrictions apply as well, the most important two are that "consonant-clusters are broken up with vowels [...] and loanwords ending in a consonant other than 'n' must end in a vowel" (Kay, 1995 : 69). The process will be shown by transcribing my surname, *Hilpisch*, according to the process utilized by the Japanese. The transcription may not be considered 'standard', however, since others might do it differently. Still, my transcription has been deemed acceptable by a native speaker of Japanese and can thus serve as an example.

In German, the name has only two syllables: *hil* and *pisch*. Both syllables pose problems for the Japanese phonology. Neither of them ends on a vowel or [*n*] and the first forms a consonant cluster with the beginning of the next syllable. This means that the syllable-final consonants have to be split away and must be treated as the onsets of syllables themselves. This leaves us with four segments: [*hi*][*l*][*pi*][*ʃ*]. The [*hi*] can be transcribed without change (ヒ), the [*l*] however, poses a problem as it not only contains a consonant unavailable in Japanese but also does not end in a vowel (it cannot, since it was no syllable to begin with). The syllable *ru* (ル) [*ru*] is the nearest equivalent – this works especially because the Japanese *r* is pronounced with a flap or trill, resembling a mixture between the English [*r*] and [*l*], and [*u*] is the vowel that is most easily silenced in Japanese pronunciation, especially in word-final positions. The next syllable, [*pi*], can be transcribed again without problem (ピ); note that *pi* is actually a variation of *hi* as is indicated by the small circle (°). This leaves the [*ʃ*], again only a consonant lacking a final vowel. Like with *l*, I choose *u* as the vowel, which gives us *schu* [*ʃu*] if we were writing this in German. A similar pronunciation is available in Japanese

36

with *shu* (シュ) [/iu/]. Thus, we have completed the transcription of the name *Hilpisch*, turning it into *hirupishu* (ヒルピシュ) [*hirupifiu*]. Thanks to the flapped [r] and the semi-silent characteristics of [*u*], this transcription proves to be as accurate as possible as it would be rendered by natural speech into something like [*hirpi/*]; the only audible change from the original then being the transformation of the [/] into [r] or [*ru*].

What takes some effort do describe at least roughly to a non-Japanese is a most natural process for native speakers. Any foreign word is easily transcribed with *katakana* and may eventually become a loanword. Since the 1980s, acceptance of foreign words grew even more, as even additional *katakana* syllables were created to ease the process of transcribing recurring syllables not available in the native Japanese syllabary, such as テ *ti* (as in *tikappu - teacup*), デ *di* (as in *disuku - disc*), チェ *chē* (as in *chēn - chain*) and ファ *fa* (as in *fakkusu - fax*) (Kay, 1995 : 69-70). Again, this shows the open-minded attitude towards foreign linguistic influences, as the Japanese are actively 'opening the doors' of their language even further.

Inclusion into Japanese syntax is usually no problem, since most of the loans are nouns and do not take inflectional endings. If they are used as verbs, adding *suru* (*to do*) usually suffices, as does adding adjectival or adverbial suffixes (*-na* and *-ni*) to turn them into adjectives and adverbs, respectively (Kay, 1995 : 72). Although loans are treated like native Japanese expressions grammatically, English words may undergo additional changes besides alteration of phonetic properties and affixation in the process of borrowing. As the addition of extra vowels into loans to fit them into the syllabic structure of Japanese regularly produces impractically long words, these are often abbreviated (Kay, 1995 : 70). Abbreviations can be produced using various morphological processes, such as backclipping (omission of final parts of the word), rarely front-clipping (omission of parts in the beginning) and blending (combining abbreviated words to a single new one). The following examples are taken from Gillian Kay (1995 : 70):

Japanese	English	Type of change
akuseru	*accel[erator]*	backclipping
omuraisu	*ome[let]+rice*	blackclipping+blending
pansuto	*pan[ty] sto[cking]*	backclipping
nisu	*[var]nish*	front-clipping

Also possible is the recombination of loanwords to new expressions with often totally different values – these would be an example of *wasei eigo*, *English-made-in-Japan*, which will be elaborated upon in section 4.2. Additionally, recombination may also take place with words from different languages (loan blending).

Japanese	Origin	Meaning	Type of change
wanpisu	*one + piece*	*dress*	recombination
opun kā	*open + car*	*convertible*	recombination
chīku dansu	*cheek + dance*	*slow dance*	recombination
haburashi	*tooth (jp) + brush*	*toothbrush*	loan blending
denwa bokkusu	*telephone (jp) + box*	*telephone box*	loan blending
wagomu	*circle (jp) + gom (dutch)*	*rubber band*	loan blending

"Many words borrowed from basic English vocabulary occur only in compound phrases" (Kay, 1995 : 71) and are usually not used on their own: *fūdo* as in *fāsuto fūdo* (*fast food*) would never be used to refer to food in general. Instead, it only refers to the specific type of food associated with typical Western 'fast food' and is limited to this semantic spectrum. This also shows the semantic change prevalent with many loanwords, which can vary "from a slight change in nuance, to a completely different meaning" (Kay, 1995 : 71). This is a natural part of borrowing, but it can lead to serious problems when the changed meanings of English loans interfere with the Standard English vocabulary students acquire in English lessons (Kay, 1995 : 74). For example, a Japanese might ask '*Do you live in a mansion?*' while actually meaning to say '*Do you live in a flat?*', since the loanword *manshon* is used in Japan to refer to higher-class flats, or apartments. A similar problem poses the lacking differentiation between loans from different languages. The loan *arubaito*, which is taken from the German expression *arbeit* (*work*) is used with the meaning *part-time job*. Oblivious to the non-English origin of the word, a student of English may say that he or she is '*going to my arbeit after school*' instead of using the English expression (*part*-time) *job*. This gives an impression of the Japanese' awareness of loanwords: as they have become an integral part of the language and although they are often recognized of foreign origin, there is not much reflection on the details. "English teachers [...] lament the occurrence of so many 'bad examples' in the daily lives of their students" (Stanlaw, 1987 : 106) but nevertheless, the corpus of English or 'English-inspired' expressions found in contemporary Japanese is still helpful in communication with Westerners, even if it might require some re-interpretation of semantic values on both sides.

4.2 *Wa-sei eigo*: English-made-in-Japan

The recombination (or re-use) of loanwords to form new terms with a completely original meaning deserves some special attention, since it has been argued that terms such as *wanpisu* (*one piece*, meaning *dress*) are not regular loanwords, but rather "English-inspired vocabulary items" (Stanlaw, 2004 : 20) or 'English-made-in-Japan'. According to Stanlaw (2004 : 20), the reasoning behind this is that many loanwords of English origin are not transparent to native speakers of English at all, because they have been created from Japanese for Japanese, using the original English term merely as an inspiration. At some point, the semantic shift has become so strong that the expression loses contact with the original and can thus no longer be considered a loanword, but instead essentially Japanese – even if the semantic value does still overlap very slightly with the original . A stronger variation of this view is that most modern terms which appear to be English loans are *wa-sei eigo*, English-made-in-Japan, and comprise an additional variety besides Japanese and Japanese English.

Another question that arises from this context is whether to consider the use of English by the Japanese to be an instance of bilingualism or rather code-switching or code-mixing. To attempt an answer a few definitions will be given with regard to this issue. According to Morrow (1987 : 54-55), code-mixing occurs intra-sententially and without any change in the speech situation, while code-switching mostly does not occur intra-sententially and is usually a reaction to a change in speech situation. Code-switching might be attempted to enable a new participant without sufficient knowledge of language A to enter the conversation by switching to language B he or she can understand as well. The Japanese use of English would fall into the category of code-mixing then, since loanwords are used intra-sententially and most Japanese without an ESL background cannot switch to English as much as necessary to enable an English-speaking participant to communicate. However, as Morrow continues, code-mixing entails bilingual competence, while code-switching does not, as can be seen from the aforementioned example. According to this, the Japanese use of English loanwords is indeed an example of bilingualism – but only if the term 'bilingual' is extended to cover speakers with English skills far below a usable level when considered on their own. The answer depends on the individual word in question. A Japanese speaker using common English loans or *wa-sei eigo* without command of the actual language may consider the loanwords Japanese items, especially when they are thoroughly assimilated – thus, neither bilingualism nor code-mixing are apparent. If the speaker is near-fluent in English as well as in Japanese and using English expressions which are not (yet) in the common vocabulary of loans, it might be considered a case of code-mixing and bilingualism, and the speaker might additionally be able to perform code-switching. The ambiguous case would be that if the word is less assimilated or the speaker has background knowledge about the English origin, it might be considered code-mixing, as there is awareness of the different code, but complete understanding is assured. There still remains the question of whether the speaker is bilingual or not, the answer depending entirely on where to set the "threshold level of bilingualism" (Morrow, 1987 : 55). Can bilingual status only be granted to speakers with decent communicative abilities, or should it also include the Japanese student whose proficiency is limited to 'Exam English'?

Borrowed English or rather English-inspired *wa-sei eigo*, bilingual or not – the Japanese use of items of English origin is not easy to classify. Stanlaw argues that the "discussion of this issue has been blurred by the adoption of a false metaphor, that is [...] 'borrowing', which in this context is both misleading and problematic" (2004 : 33). He suggests instead analyzing "the motivations and purposes supporting the creation of English words and phrases within Japanese society" (2004 : 34), which will be discussed in section 4.3 in more detail.

4.3 Reasons for borrowing

The simplest reason for borrowing is of course that a foreign word may cover a concept formerly totally unknown in one's own culture. In Japan, this was the case when the country suddenly opened to the West and a surge of cultural items had to be dealt with and also had to be named, so that nowadays a Japanese customer can tell a shop owner that he is looking for a *nekutai* for himself and a *wanpisu* for his wife. One has to keep in mind that the whole process of evolving from a secluded island nation to a global player took only about one century, and the language had to keep up with the many innovations brought from the outside. Borrowing was the simplest way to include the new concepts both into the language and into culture. Kay (1995 : 73) summarizes the benefits of borrowing via ear through the *katakana* syllabary in favour of the invention of native expressions as follows:

> "Katakana [...] physically separates loanwords from those of native or ancient Chinese origin by representing them in a conspicuously different script. Keeping foreign words compartmentalized in this way allows the language to gain maximum benefit from their addition to the lexical pool, while protecting the native vocabulary from change. The orthographical separation of loanwords thus enables Japan to develop a Western vocabulary to accompany and assist its Westernization, without threatening the basic integrity of the native language."

40

The separation of loans from the native language lessens the threat on cultural identity posed by foreign influences. At the same time, this makes it possible to use loanwords to express already present concepts in new ways and often more freely, since the loans do not carry as many traditional undertones as native Japanese expressions (Kay, 1995 : 74). This makes them especially attractive to arts and marketing, as shown in chapter 3.4, but is also useful in daily conversation to add different nuances to the discourse beyond the lexical level.

Hayashi (et al., 1995) have conducted research on a cognitive perspective of reasons to use a loan instead of a synonymous native expression, and how loanwords can be vital for a speaker to reach his or her goal in discourse. They conclude that "the data showed that English loanwords are used with purpose, not only within but beyond sentence levels and as an integral parts of discourse goal" (Hayashi, et al., 1995 : 64). Using examples from common discourse situations, they differentiate between 5 different purposes for which English loanwords can be utilized to achieve a specific communicative goal (Hayashi, et al., 1995 : 59-63). First, there is *Explanation*, where a foreign expression is used to explain ideas or objects which are yet unknown to traditional Japanese culture. This is the most common use, since it is very often the case that a new concept is more easily and also readily understood when clad in a descriptive foreign loanword. The second purpose is *Elaboration*, where a loan is used to provide additional information on a new concept to fill gaps left by not completely accurate native expressions. Here, the loan is used in addition to other (native) expressions, not on its own. The third purpose is *Backgrounding*, where speakers utilize loans to convey background information. This can be done when the loan evokes an additional image the native alternative is lacking, thus changing the context to one in which the speaker feels his or her ideas are conveyed more appropriately. Loans can also be used for *Exemplification*, when a speaker wants to exemplify an idea by giving a similar Western concept which is already known through a loan. Finally, there is *Generalization*, where a loan may convey a broader range of semantic implications than possible native alternatives, thus leaving the statement vaguer by including the meanings of multiple Japanese words in one loan.

What can be seen from all these five purposes is that loans are quite often used deliberately, with intentions beyond the simple ideas of 'being Western' (and thus modern or sophisticated) and 'naming things' (instead of devising Japanese expressions). Of course, especially the 'modern ring' of English has its uses in advertising and the media as this paper has shown, but there is much more to it than just this. English has become a tool for Japanese speakers to express themselves in ways not possible (or at least more difficult) in native Japanese expressions only. One example would be various notions of individualism, which are difficult to convey in Standard Japanese without sounding egocentric (Stanlaw, 1987 : 99). Expressions like *mai-hoomu* (*my home*) and *mai-puraibashi* (*my privacy*) reflect a change in the Japanese' self-awareness, giving more priority to the private environment – the Japanese language, having evolved in a collective environment, is not fit for conveying such concepts without trouble. In fact, even the very basic term *watashi no* (*my*) has a strongly selfish ring to it, which is why this pronoun is mostly avoided whenever possible. Similarly, notions of romance or sex are often conveyed using English vocabulary in favour of native Japanese terms, "which sometimes are even non-existent for the topic in question" (Stanlaw, 1987 : 99). Generally, English expressions are easier to use in controversial contexts, since they either convey 'differentness' from the native alternative (and thus a new approach to the topic) or less sub textual ballast, avoiding problems with traditional images attached to native terms.

English loans are absolutely necessary in the modern Japanese society, since they are utilized in almost every aspect of life, and living without them has become unimaginable. English has followed Chinese in its footsteps as a vehicle for innovation in Japan. There are thousands of concepts, both material and immaterial, that depend on their corresponding loanwords not only as a signifier but also benefit from the various new undertones – and sometimes even the lack of the same.

5. Conclusion

Japan can look back on a vivid history of language contact with multiple cultures, beginning with other Asian nations such as China, followed by encounters with the great European trading nations to their most recent visitors who brought them into contact with the English language. These engagements have one thing in common: the Japanese always made sure to take in everything from the other culture that might be beneficial to them, build on that and make it into something of their own, while always retaining their national identity.

After the Chinese writing system, a milestone in cultural development, the Japanese remained open-minded towards foreign influences. Fearing a downfall of original Japanese culture, the pre-*Meiji* regime secluded Japan for two centuries, only to face a strong, advanced West immediately afterwards. In a hurry to catch up with the rest of the Globe, Japan put much effort into teaching English to its citizens, while at the same time innumerable loanwords entered the language to describe the new, fancy and innovative concepts imported from the West. English obtained both practical and prestigious value for the citizens, and there was a general agreement about English and the West being the future of Japan. This continued for decades and English became as important for Japan as was Chinese many centuries ago, even though the English language lost some of its prestige, accompanied by a rising self-confidence the Japanese had in themselves and their language. The English loans developed into new forms inside their new environment, leading to what is often called English-made-in-Japan, and their importance grew so much that nowadays, items of English origin are a vital part of Japanese language and culture, co-existing on an equal level with native Japanese terms.

What makes this process so special is that the Japanese used a foreign language to actively expand their own, together with their culture, to fit into a new, changed world. Simultaneously and only seemingly paradoxical, this helped them to retain their cultural identity. They took foreign influences, and instead of being overwhelmed, they devised methods to assimilate them, thus turning them into something very Japanese.

Bibliography

Coulmas, Florian. 1989. Japanese Writing. *The Writing Systems of the World.* Oxford : Basil Blackwell Ltd., 1989, pp. 122-136.

Dettmer, Hans A. 1973. *Grundzüge der Geschichte Japans.* Darmstadt : Wissenschaftliche Buchgesellschaft, 1973.

Doitsu Center Ltd. 2006. *Japanisch im Sauseschritt.* Tokyo : Kodansha International Ltd., 2006.

Graham, Richard. 2009. Genki English - What to teach? [Online] 2009. [Cited: 07 12, 2009.] http://genkienglish.net/whatteach.htm.

Hayashi, Takuo and Hayashi, Reiko. 1995. A cognitive study of English loanwords in Japanese discourse. *World Englishes Vol. 14, No. 1.* 1995, pp. 55-66.

Ike, Minoru. 1995. A historical review of English in Japan (1600-1880). *World Englishes Vol. 14, No. 1.* 1995, pp. 3-11.

JET-Programme. 2009. Official Homepage. [Online] 2009. [Cited: 07 12, 2009.] http://www.jetprogramme.org/e/introduction/index.html.

Kay, Gillian. 1995. English loanwords in Japanese. *World Englishes Vol. 14, No. 1.* 1995, pp. 67-76.

Koike, Ikuo and Tanaka, Harumi. 1995. English in foreign langauge education policy in Japan:. *World Englishes Vol. 14, No. 1.* 1995, pp. 13-25.

Loveday, Leo J. 1996. *Language Contact in Japan: a socio-linguistic history.* Oxford : Oxford University Press, 1996.

Miura, Akira. 1979. *English Loanwords in Japanese: A Selection.* Tokyo : Charles E. Tuttle Company, 1979.

Morrow, Phillip R. 1995. English in a Japanese company: The case of Toshiba. *World Englishes Vol. 14, No. 1.* 1995, pp. 87-98.

—. 1987. The users and uses of English in Japan. *World Englishes Vol. 6, No. 1.* 1987, pp. 49-62.

Nishiyama, Sen. 1995. Speaking English with a Japanese mind. *World Englishes Vol. 14, No. 1.* 1995, pp. 27-36.

Reischauer, Edwin O. and Jansen, Marius B. 1995. *The Japanese Today: Change and Continuity (Enlarged Edition).* Cambridge : Harvard University Press, 1995.

Reischauer, Edwin O. 1977. *The Japanese.* Cambridge : The Belknap Press of Harvard University Press, 1977.

Sebba, Mark. 1997. *Contact Languages: Pidgins and Creoles.* London : Macmillan Press, 1997.

Stanlaw, James. 1987. Japanese and English: borrowing and contact. *World Englishes Vol. 6, No. 2.* 1987, pp. 93-109.

—. **2004.** *Japanese English: Language and Culture Contact.* Aberdeen/Hong Kong : Hong Kong University Press, 2004.

Takashi, Kyoko. 1990. A sociolinguistic analysis of English borrowings in Japanese advertising texts. *World Englishes Vol. 9, No. 3.* 1990, pp. 327-341.

Tanaka, Sachiko Oda and Tanaka, Harumi. 1995. A survey of Japanese sources on the use of English in Japan. *World Englishes Vol. 14, No. 1.* 1995, pp. 117-135.

Tables, Figures and Pictures

CPSIA information can be obtained at www.ICGtesting.com
Printed in the USA
236310LV00002B/164/P